Copywork with the Masters

Copywork with Shakespeare

*Annotated Selctions from Shakespeare's
A Comedy of Errors and Richard III*

Edited with notes by Dr Kat Patrick

ABOUT THE EDITOR

Kat Patrick is originally from Texas, but has lived in the Cotswold area of England for almost half her life. She studied for her BA at Southwestern University in Georgetown, Texas, her MA at Durham University in the UK, her PhD at the University of Delaware back in the States, and finally, received her teaching degree from South Bank University in England.

Her area of focus is seventeenth-century literary history of England, but because of teaching in UK secondary schools and at university-level in the US, she has covered nearly every era of literature during her teaching career. Moreover, as a homeschooler of four children, she has delved into just about every subject under the sun — from Japanese cooking to rose gardening, Roman mosaic design to kitchen chemistry, honey bee physiology to breeding tropical fish.

More recently, she has expanded her homeschooling venture by teaching online courses for teens all over the world through her company called Dreaming Spires Home Learning. Not only does she offer four years' worth of high-level English courses, she is gradually roping in all of her professional friends to offer courses in Ancient and Modern History, Sciences, and Spanish, with more to come!

She's a dedicated follower of the Charlotte Mason method, a liberal arts approach to education that is characterised by:

- short lessons
- use of living books as opposed to dry textbooks

- employing narration, dictation, and copywork for Language Arts skills
- nature study
- art- and music-appreciation
- free afternoons to work on handicrafts, outdoor pursuits, or other personal interests

You can see the influence of Charlotte Mason in not only her online courses at Dreaming Spires, but in the whole conception of this book about copyable quotes from Shakespeare. More about this in "Ye Olde Introduction".

Hope you enjoy this book!

Kat blogs about the Charlotte Mason lifestyle on www.boyschooling.blogspot.com, and about high school home-schooling at www.dreamingspireshomelearning.com (.co.uk for UK-based teens).

OTHER WAYS TO CONNECT WITH KAT ARE:

facebook.com/dreamingspireshomelearning

twitter.com/dreaminspiresHL

instagram.com/dreaming_spires_home_learning

YE OLDE INTRODUCTION

You hold in your hands a true labour of love — a selection of speeches from some of Shakespeare's favourite plays, intended for use as copywork in your homeschool curriculum.

When I use the word "copywork", I mean a skill that forms one of the hallmarks of the Charlotte Mason method. Sometimes known as "transcription", the process by which students copy directly from an excellent piece of literature, is - to my mind - akin to the stage of an apprentice painter, when he painstakingly copies the brushstrokes, proportions, and composition of a work by a Rembrandt, a Van Gogh, or a Degas.

It's not a difficult skill, or particularly time-consuming: just ten minutes a day is all it takes. However, the slow burn of ingesting good punctuation, spelling, vocabulary, sentence structures, and such enormous control over words, is a proven path to excellent writing.

You don't even need to buy a curriculum for the purpose. Just pick up any Dickens or Bronte or Eliot, and you've made an excellent choice of a literary Old Master to learn from.

This book, however, is a bit special. It's selections from Shakespeare, and unlike novels from the 18th- and 19th-centuries, the plays that The Bard wrote (in the Elizabethan era) are just a little bit more alien to our language and style of today, and so, he can be hard to "get into" without a bit of help.

That help comes in three main forms here:

- selections and not unexpurgated lines from the play. This is so students are exposed to the best bits of the play, and spend precious copywork time in neither the rude parts nor the throw-away exchanges of "Fie" and "Yes, my Lord," etc.
- explanation, background, and summary for every selection. This is so students don't feel as though they are simply copying heiroglyphics or Greek, but words that belong to a plot-line that's easy to understand.
- additional observations, memories, and moments from plays I've seen in performance. This is so students are reminded that these were works meant for the stage, and also, to give insight into how many choices go into each director's interpretation: from casting to costuming to setting.

One final point: the selections in this book are not modernized, but are kept in Shakespeare's Elizabethan English. Although it may seem unfamiliar, it is, in fact, modern English — or, more accurately, Early Modern English. I mean, you might not exactly understand what Shakespeare means by "I'll utter what my sorrow gives me leave," but there's no doubt that every word in it is one we are likely to come across today.[1]

Compare that line to Old English ("Hwæt! We Gar-Dena in geardagum" - opening line of Beowulf) or Middle English ("When that Aprille with his shoures soote" - opening line of Canterbury Tales). These works are usually modernized so students can understand and enjoy the stories without getting bogged down in translating the words themselves. While this happens to some extent with Shakespeare, it's usually because he's simply unfamiliar rather than unintelligible.

So, to re-cap: this book is selections of un-modernized Shakespearean speeches with explanatory notes, intended to be used for copywork.

I'm also hoping that this book will not only strengthen your children's mechanics and stylistics of good writing, but will also give them a taste for Shakespeare that will lead to reading more plays and seeing more productions.

Afer all, if "all the world's a stage",[2] then it seems fitting that your students learn to play their own parts in it!

MORE ABOUT COPYWORK

Earlier, I explained what copywork was, but I want to reiterate how students should undertake copywork as part of their daily studies.

There are four steps:

1. Choose a book to copy from (this one is a good one 😊)
2. Open your notebook, blank journal, composition book, etc.
3. Pick up a pen, pencil, fountain pen, etc.
4. Set a timer for ten minutes and start to copy from the book, word for word, until the timer stops.

One of the great advantages of the task is that, while students are learning all the Language Arts skills of writing well, they are also learning to hold words in their minds while they look from the original passage to their notebooks. At first, they may be able to hold only one or two words, but with practice, that mind-memory will contain more and more words, until whole lines can be transferred over. This is a useful skill to have for life, not just for English.

Further, in our copy/paste world, taking accurate notes is a lost art. Copywork teaches students to concentrate on the minutiae of writing — every jot and tittle.

Not bad for an activity that's little more than sitting down to write for ten minutes!

––––––––––

1. Basically, Egeon is saying, "I'll tell you as much of my story as my sorrow allows me to tell you." — Comedy of Errors.

2. This famous quote comes from As You Like It.

APPROXIMATE CHRONOLOGY OF
SHAKESPEARE'S PLAYS

Some of the surviving texts were part of the "First Folio," published in 1623. The "First Folio" included some thirty-six plays, and the editor took some care in the selection and accuracy of his texts, or at least more care than those texts that were part of the quartos published in other years.

†*Some of the surviving texts were part of a "bad" quarto printing. A bad quarto is a copy of the play that a disloyal actor would recreate from memory and then submit for publication in a rival publishing house without the consent of the author. These bad quartos are often grossly inaccurate, but many contain useful stage directions lacking in the original text.*

Date Work

1589-90 1 Henry VI (revised 1594-95)*

1590-91 2 Henry VI (published 1594)*†

1590-91 3 Henry VI (published 1595)*†

1592-94 The Comedy of Errors*

1592-93 Richard III ("bad" quarto 1597)*†

1592-94 Titus Andronicus (first published 1594)†

1593-94 The Taming of the Shrew (1594)*†

1594 The Two Gentlemen of Verona*

1594-95 Love's Labor's Lost (probably revised in 1595 or 1597; published 1598)

1594-96 King John*

1595 Richard II (published 1597)

1595-96 Romeo and Juliet (published 1599; 1597†)

1595-96 A Midsummer Night's Dream

1596-97 The Merchant of Venice (published in 1600)

1597-1601 The Merry Wives of Windsor* (revised 1600-01; 1602†)

1597 1 Henry IV (published 1598)

1598 2 Henry IV (published 1600)

1598-99 Much Ado About Nothing

1599 Henry V (published 1600)

1599 Julius Caesar

1599 As You Like It

1600-01 Hamlet (published 1604; 1603†)

1601-02 Twelfth Night*

1601-02 Troilus and Cressida (published 1609)

1602-03 All's Well That Ends Well*

1604 Othello (published 1622)

1604 Measure for Measure*

1605 King Lear (published 1608)

1606 Macbeth*

1606-07 Antony and Cleopatra*

1607-08 Timon of Athens (published 1609)

1607-08 Coriolanus*

1607-08 Pericles

1609-10 Cymbeline*

1610-11 The Winter's Tale*

1611 The Tempest*

1612-13 Henry VIII

1612-13 Cardenio (a lost play)

1613 The Two Noble Kinsmen, with Fletcher (published 1634)

Information taken from
https://web.cn.edu/kwheeler/documents/Chronological_Shake_C
anon.pdf

COMEDY OF ERRORS

This play is considered one of Shakespeare's earliest. Known to have been performed in 1594, it may have been performed a year or two earlier, though the play isn't named as such. It was certainly penned before 1594, and definitely marks his first comedy even if it doesn't antedate the three Henry VI plays.

Basically, there is a young man named Antipholus who, more or less since birth, has had the same serving man, Dromio. They were both separated from their twin brothers in a tragic shipwreck when they were but babies. They have heard that their long-lost brothers may be in Ephesus, so they travel from Syracuse to see if they can locate them.

This is where the mayhem begins, because you see, the lost brothers are also called Antipholus and Dromio, and are identical to their twins in looks, too. When Antipholus from Syracuse arrives in Ephesus, he tells Dromio from Syracuse to deposit money in a bank; shortly afterward, he comes across Dromio from Ephesus who is looking to fetch his master - Antipholus from Ephesus - back to dinner at the behest of his wife.

Antipholus from Syracuse wonders where the money is that he gave his servant... Dromio from Ephesus has no idea about any money, but instead, is on an errand to bring his master back home for dinner. Of course, Antipholus from Syracuse - a stranger to town - has no idea what this serving-man is talking about. A wife? The stories of magic and mayhem in Ephesus are true! And on and on and on!

There's an additional subplot about their father having followed them to Ephesus, and he falls afoul of rules that bar entry to people from Syracuse, meaning that he either has to pay a fine of 1000 marks, or be put to death.

Of course, all works out in the end. It's a comedy, isn't it?? A delightfully funny story, full of mistaken identity and often physical comedy, its conclusion is so lovely that I often cry for joy at the end.

I find the best way to keep the characters straight is to call them Antipholus 1 and Dromio 1 for those from Syracuse, and Antipholus 2 and Dromio 2 from Ephesus. When you see a live performance, however, there is rarely any confusion for the audience, but the faces and behaviours of those on stage are hilarious.

SELECTIONS FROM COMEDY OF ERRORS

COPYWORK 1

DUKE

Merchant of Syracusa, plead no more.

I am not partial to infringe our laws:

It hath in solemn synods been decreed,

Both by the Syracusians and ourselves,

T' admit no traffic to our fighting towns:

Nay, more, if any, born at Ephesus

Be seen at Syracusian marts and fairs;

Again, if any Syracusian born

Come to the bay of Ephesus, he dies,

His goods confiscate to the duke's dispose;

Unless a thousand marks be levied,

To quit the penalty and to ransom him.

Thy substance, valu'd at the highest rate,

Cannot amount unto a hundred marks;

Therefore, by law thou art condemn'd to die. (I.i.5-27)³

⤳

It's at the very beginning of the play that we see the father's plot-point unfold. Namely, the father of Antipholus of Syracuse, Egeon, has come to Ephesus to look for his son (who has come to look for his long-lost brother), but has fallen afoul of the law as soon as he has arrived: both governments have agreed that any citizens of the opposing town will be arrested and either put to death, or pay a fine of 1000 marks. Egeon can't pay, so he is doomed to die.

---

3. These designations in brackets after the speech tell you with act and scene you'll find the speech. In this case, it's Act 1, scene 1. It's usual to delineate plays with a big Roman numeral for an act, and a little Roman numeral for a scene, and Arabic numerals for the line numbers. That's because few plays in written form will match up page numbers between editions, but their Act, scene, and line numbers usually be the same in whatever book you have.

SELECTIONS FROM COMEDY OF ERRORS

COPYWORK 2 (CAN BE BROKEN UP INTO TWO OR THREE SESSIONS)

EGEON

A heavier task could not have been imposed

Than I to speak my griefs unspeakable:

Yet, that the world may witness that my end

Was wrought by nature, not by vile offence,

I'll utter what my sorrows give me leave.

In Syracusa was I born, and wed

Unto a woman, happy but for me,

And by me, had not our hap been bad.

With her I lived in joy; our wealth increased

By prosperous voyages I often made

To Epidamnum; till my factor's death

And the great care of goods at random left

Drew me from kind embracements of my spouse:

From whom my absence was not six months old

Before herself, almost at fainting under

The pleasing punishment that women bear,

Had made provision for her following me

And soon and safe arrived where I was.

There had she not been long, but she became

A joyful mother of two goodly sons;

And, which was strange, the one so like the other,

As could not be distinguish'd but by names.

That very hour, and in the self-same inn,

A meaner woman was delivered

Of such a burden, male twins, both alike:

Those,—for their parents were exceeding poor,—

I bought and brought up to attend my sons.

My wife, not meanly proud of two such boys,

Made daily motions for our home return:

Unwilling I agreed. Alas! too soon,

We came aboard.

A league from Epidamnum had we sail'd,

Before the always wind-obeying deep

Gave any tragic instance of our harm:

But longer did we not retain much hope;

For what obscured light the heavens did grant

Did but convey unto our fearful minds

A doubtful warrant of immediate death;

Which though myself would gladly have embraced,

Yet the incessant weepings of my wife,

Weeping before for what she saw must come,

And piteous plainings of the pretty babes,

That mourn'd for fashion, ignorant what to fear,

Forced me to seek delays for them and me.

And this it was, for other means was none:

The sailors sought for safety by our boat,

And left the ship, then sinking-ripe, to us:

My wife, more careful for the latter-born,

Had fasten'd him unto a small spare mast,

Such as seafaring men provide for storms;

To him one of the other twins was bound,

Whilst I had been like heedful of the other:

The children thus disposed, my wife and I,

Fixing our eyes on whom our care was fix'd,

Fasten'd ourselves at either end the mast;

And floating straight, obedient to the stream,

Was carried towards Corinth, as we thought.

At length the sun, gazing upon the earth,

Dispersed those vapours that offended us;

And by the benefit of his wished light,

The seas wax'd calm, and we discovered

Two ships from far making amain to us,

Of Corinth that, of Epidaurus this:

But ere they came,—O, let me say no more!

Gather the sequel by that went before. (I.i.33-97)

~

Clear as mud? Egeon explains to the Duke why he has risked his life by coming to Ephesus. Basically, he's looking for Antipholus 1, but we get more back-story than that! Egeon is a merchant who has always traveled a lot, and many years ago, his wife joined him on one of his voyages. She gave birth to twins who looked exactly the same, and as fate would have it, a poor woman also delivered twins at the same time. Egeon bought these boys at birth to be servants for his twins. On the voyage home, there was a storm and the ship sank. Egeon and his wife lashed the children to a mast. As the storm subsided, they saw two ships. In a further speech (not included in this book), Egeon explains the mast was broken in two by a rock, and his wife's half, along with the boy and his baby servant, were saved by a boat bound for Corinth. Meanwhile, Egeon and his two charges were picked up by a different boat, and for more than twenty years, he has had no news of his wife and other son.

SELECTIONS FROM COMEDY OF ERRORS

COPYWORK 3

ANTOPHOLOS OF SYRACUSE

A heavier task could not have been imposed

Upon my life, by some device or other

The villain is o'er-raught of all my money.

They say this town is full of cozenage,

As, nimble jugglers that deceive the eye,

Dark-working sorcerers that change the mind,

Soul-killing witches that deform the body,

Disguised cheaters, prating mountebanks,

And many such-like liberties of sin:

If it prove so, I will be gone the sooner.

I'll to the Centaur, to go seek this slave:

I greatly fear my money is not safe. (I.ii.259-270)

∼

It's our first look at the state of confusion we'll witness in this play: Antipholus of Syracuse has just arrived in Ephesus and given his servant, Dromio, a bag full of money to deposit in a bank. Then he sees Dromio from Ephesus, his servant's identical twin brother, and asks him about the money. Of course, Dromio 2 doesn't know anything about it, so runs away. As Ephesus has a reputation for magic and sorcery, Antipholus 1 becomes more and more convinced that he's a victim of some supernatural confusion. The speech ends with his saying he's going back to the inn, the Centaur, where he can interrogate Dromio about the money some more.

SELECTIONS FROM COMEDY OF ERRORS

COPYWORK 4

ADRIANA

How ill agrees it with your gravity

To counterfeit thus grossly with your slave,

Abetting him to thwart me in my mood!

Be it my wrong you are from me exempt,

But wrong not that wrong with a more contempt.

Come, I will fasten on this sleeve of thine:

Thou art an elm, my husband, I a vine,

Whose weakness, married to thy stronger state,

Makes me with thy strength to communicate:

If aught possess thee from me, it is dross,

Usurping ivy, brier, or idle moss;

Who, all for want of pruning, with intrusion

Infect thy sap and live on thy confusion. (II.ii.557-569)

~

Adriana is the wife of Antipholus of Ephesus. She has been waiting for her husband to arrive for lunch but it's Antipholus of Syracuse whom she comes upon in the streets. She thinks his claims that he doesn't know her are just a cruel joke, and she says that his strength gives her, as his wife, the strength to complain to him. She says the distractions that have been keeping her from him are worthless like weeds, and should be cut off so they don't get into his system and infect him. Note her rhyming couplets here starting from "exempt".

SELECTIONS FROM COMEDY OF ERRORS

COPYWORK 5

BALTHAZAR [a merchant, friend of Antipholus 2]

Have patience, sir; O, let it not be so!

Herein you war against your reputation

And draw within the compass of suspect

The unviolated honour of your wife.

Once this,—your long experience of her wisdom,

Her sober virtue, years and modesty,

Plead on her part some cause to you unknown:

And doubt not, sir, but she will well excuse

Why at this time the doors are made against you.

Be ruled by me: depart in patience,

And let us to the Tiger all to dinner,

And about evening come yourself alone

To know the reason of this strange restraint.

If by strong hand you offer to break in

Now in the stirring passage of the day,

A vulgar comment will be made of it,

And that supposed by the common rout

Against your yet ungalled estimation

That may with foul intrusion enter in

And dwell upon your grave when you are dead;

For slander lives upon succession,

For ever housed where it gets possession.

(This conversation continues on the next page for selection 6)

SELECTIONS FROM COMEDY OF ERRORS

COPYWORK 6

ANTIPHOLOS OF EPHESUS

You have prevailed: I will depart in quiet,

And, in despite of mirth, mean to be merry.

I know a wench of excellent discourse,

Pretty and witty; wild, and yet, too, gentle:

There will we dine. This woman that I mean,

My wife—but, I protest, without desert—

Hath oftentimes upbraided me withal:

To her will we to dinner.

[To Angelo, the goldsmith]

Get you home

And fetch the chain; by this I know 'tis made:

Bring it, I pray you, to the Porpentine;

For there's the house: that chain will I bestow—

Be it for nothing but to spite my wife—

Upon mine hostess there: good sir, make haste.

Since mine own doors refuse to entertain me,

I'll knock elsewhere, to see if they'll disdain me.
(III.i.720-758)

~

This is our first glimpse of Antipholus of Ephesus. We learn that he has invited the merchant, Balthazar, to dine with him at his home, but when they try to enter the house, it's locked and no one will let them in. (The reason, of course, is that Antipholus 1 is inside already, having been mistaken for her husband, Antipholus 2, by Adriana). Antipholus 2 is threatening to break the door down, but Balthazar urges him to be patient, since this is very unusual behaviour for Adriana and a commotion in broad daylight will soil their reputations. He suggests they go instead to eat at the Tiger, but Antipholus wants to eat at a different place, owned by a woman with whom he flirts a lot. He then tells Angelo, the goldsmith, to go fetch the gold chain that he'd ordered as a present for Adriana, but take it to this woman at the Porpentine inn instead as payback for his wife's rudeness to him.

SELECTIONS FROM COMEDY OF ERRORS

COPYWORK 7

ADRIANA

May it please your grace, Antipholus, my husband,

Whom I made lord of me and all I had,

At your important letters,—this ill day

A most outrageous fit of madness took him;

That desperately he hurried through the street,

With him his bondman, all as mad as he—

Doing displeasure to the citizens

By rushing in their houses, bearing thence

Rings, jewels, any thing his rage did like.

Once did I get him bound and sent him home,

Whilst to take order for the wrongs I went,

That here and there his fury had committed.

Anon, I wot not by what strong escape,

He broke from those that had the guard of him;

And with his mad attendant and himself,

Each one with ireful passion, with drawn swords,

Met us again and madly bent on us,

Chased us away; till, raising of more aid,

We came again to bind them. Then they fled

Into this abbey, whither we pursued them:

And here the abbess shuts the gates on us

And will not suffer us to fetch him out,

Nor send him forth that we may bear him hence.

Therefore, most gracious duke, with thy command

Let him be brought forth and borne hence for help.
(V.i.136-160)

Adriana tries to sum up all that has happened as far as she understands it — her husband and his servant, both acting crazy, were tied up at home. Next thing she knows, they've escaped and are hiding from her in the abbey. It's a speech full of dramatic irony, for we the audience know that Antipholus 1 and Dromio 1 are still tied up in the house, while Antipholus 2 and Dromio 2 are hiding in the abbey. What we don't know is what happens next!

SELECTIONS FROM COMEDY OF ERRORS

COPYWORK 8:

ABBESS

Whoever bound him, I will loose his bonds

And gain a husband by his liberty.—

Speak, old Egeon, if thou be'st the man

That hadst a wife once called Emilia,

That bore thee at a burden two fair sons.

O, if thou be'st the same Egeon, speak,

And speak unto the same Emilia.

DUKE

Why, here begins his morning story right;

These two Antipholuses, these two so like,

And these two Dromios, one in semblance—

Besides her urging of her wreck at sea—

These are the parents to these children,

Which accidentally are met together.

EGEON

If I dream not, thou art Emilia.

If thou art she, tell me where is that son

That floated with thee on the fatal raft?

ABBESS

By men of Epidamnum he and I

And the twin Dromio all were taken up;

But by and by rude fishermen of Corinth

By force took Dromio and my son from them

And me they left with those of Epidamnum.

What then became of them I cannot tell;

I to this fortune that you see me in. (V.i.342-364)

Now all is revealed: Antipholus 1 and 2, Dromio 1 and 2, Egeon, the Duke, Adriana, and all, learn that the abbess is the long-lost mother of the twins, the wife of Egeon, and now she unravels all the knots of Ephesus's magical day. Bags of money are returned to their rightful owners, necklaces to their proper love, and the Duke frees Egeon without paying a fine, I'm almost tempted to say all's well that ends well, but that's another play!

SELECTIONS FROM COMEDY OF
ERRORS: THE FINAL LINES

COPYWORK 9

DROMIO OF EPHESUS

Methinks you are my glass, and not my brother:

I see by you I am a sweet-faced youth.

Will you walk in to see their gossiping?

DROMIO OF SYRACUSE

Not I, sir. You are my elder.

DROMIO OF EPHESUS

That's a question. How shall we try it?

DROMIO OF SYRACUSE

We'll draw cuts for the signior. Till then, lead thou first.

DROMIO OF EPHESUS

Nay, then, thus:

We came into the world like brother and brother,

And now let's go hand in hand, not one before another.
(V.1.422-430)

~

The final lines in the play are spoken by the Dromio twins. They reiterate how alike they seem, so much that they can't tell themselves apart, but more than that, by leaving the stage side by side, they underline the harmony that has been re-established at the end.

COMEDY OF ERRORS: THE
PRODUCTIONS

I've seen two productions of this play, one at the Rutland Open Air Theatre performed by the Stamford Shakespeare Company in 1993, and the other in a village hall in Henley-in-Arden by the traveling troupe known as Rain or Shine Theatre Company in 2013.

The most memorable part of the former play was that we saw it in June, when the willow trees were shedding their fluffy seed capsules. Being an open air theatre in a thick wood, the fluff was an inch thick or more on the stage, so any scuffling or dancing or vigorous movements would send the fluff into air. They would catch the light and make the scene look like a snow globe.

Try to imagine the final exchange with the two Dromios. They were dressed a bit like modern clowns: short, black trousers, red-striped shirts, and big afro wigs. As they danced together, they headed straight off the back of the stage where a path disappears into the trees, snow-globe willow fluffies sparkling in the multi-coloured stage lights. It was as though the whole play really was a sort of magical dream.

The Rain or Shine play had its own kind of magic — a cast who interacted with the crowd, made full use of physical comedy, and because they used a pirate theme throughout, their piratey songs and piratey accents were hilarious. We were amazed by a small cast that could double-up parts in the blink of an eye. This was my younger children's first performance of live Shakespeare. We arrived early for an indoor picnic,[4] grabbing a front-row table so we'd miss none of the action. Little did we know we were in the firing line for the buckets of water!

---

4. The original plan to perform the play in a garden outdoors was altered due to weather.

RICHARD III

This play was written about the same time as our previous one, Comedy of Errors, but couldn't be more different.

First of all, it's part of a group of plays which dealt with Britain's historical past, thus the crossed-swords icon of this copywork book's history plays.[5] You'll see the three prequels to Richard III being listed in our chronology as Shakespeare's very earliest plays - the trilogy about Henry VI's reign during the Wars of the Roses (c. 1455-1485).

The four plays together are known as the First Tetrology, or series of four plays that deal with the time period. Probably it's more appropriate to call them a "cycle" of plays, where each play can be performed separately, but together, they form a bigger picture.

Of the four, the final installment, Richard III, is by far the best and most-often performed of the series.

As an aside, the Second Tetralogy is the Henriad Cycle starting with Richard II, followed by Henry IV Part 1, Henry IV Part 2, and Henry V. These four plays take place chronologically earlier in English history, but were written a few years later than the First Tetralogy.

We know that <u>Richard III</u> must have been performed in the 1590s, but there is no record of it until 1633 when Charles I attended it at the royal court. We also know that the earliest portrayals of our title character would have been undertaken by Richard Burbage, one of Shakespeare's favourite actors from his troupe, and probably the very person that the author had in mind when writing the role.

Speaking of character, let's be clear about one thing: Richard III of Shakespeare's play is a construct. The real man, as far as we know, was not hideously deformed as Shakespeare describes him, nor responsible for most of the deaths and murders that Shakespeare blames him for in the play. In fact, archaeologists recently located and exhumed the body of the real king when it was discovered under a car park in Leicester, and while it showed signs of scoliosis (curvature of the spine), it was not as extreme as to have caused the hunchback that Shakespeare gives him.

Even though Richard was not a hunchback in real life, the Shakespearean character we read about - the plotting, two-faced, over-confident king - is the enduring one, and is perennially one of the most sought-after roles in the theatre still today.

So what's the story-line of the play? Remember that this play is the fourth in a series, so most of the background has been covered in the three plays before, charting the rise and fall of King Henry VI and how he ended up losing the throne to his cousin, Edward IV, Richard's older brother.

At the start of the play, Edward has just been crowned king for the SECOND time, because although Edward deposed Henry VI in 1461, Henry managed to come back in 1470 (with the help of his wife and some of Edward's followers-turned-traitors) and wrested it from Edward again. The "readeption" of Henry, as this is called, lasted only 6 months, so in 1471, Edward invaded from Europe, and at the Battle of Tewkesbury, dispatched with most of his enemies, including Henry VI's son and heir, confusingly also named Edward. Shortly after this defeat, King Henry died in the Tower under mysterious circumstances. In the play, Richard claims to have carried out the murder, though in real life, it's thought that Edward IV ordered it and Richard was merely one of the bystanders.

I guess you could say that the beginning of the play is supposed to represent a kind of "peace at last" for the bloody and prolonged Wars of the Roses. The red rose of the Lancasters was crumpled and basically dead except for one distant relative who had fled to France (the future Henry VII), and the white rose was firmly on the throne with a healthy depth of heirs: Edward IV had two sons and a daughter, as well as two brothers.

It looked as though the white rose of the Yorks was going to start a dynasty.

The only problem was that this rose had a nasty, hidden thorn: Richard, Duke of Gloucester. From the very first lines of the play, we learn that he is a bitter and unhappy guy whose capacity for enjoying peace is basically nil. He blames it on his misshapen body, as though that means his mind, too, is misshapen and "bent" toward evil.

He tells us from the beginning that he's going to cause havoc, and his next victim is his own brother, George the Duke of Clarence. If you think that's a low blow, then you ain't seen nothing yet! He goes to the funeral of Henry VI and sees the grieving widow of Henry's son, Edward, only to flirt with her until she agrees to marry him, and lowest of all, after his brother Edward IV dies, he agrees to fetch his two young nephews from their country castle and bring them back to London in order to crown the elder one (also called

Edward!) in his father's place, but his real purpose is to lock the pair in the Tower of London and conspire to have them murdered.

But wait! It can get even worse! His piece de resistance. he ends up poisoning his wife because he decides that marrying his niece, Edward IV's daughter, would be a politic move for securing his claim to the throne.

Eventually, it all unravels. That little distant cousin who has only a tenuous claim to the throne through his mother - the cousin that has been hiding in France this whole time - turns up on Britain's shores with an army. On the eve of battle, Richard is visited by the ghosts of all he has laid waste during the course of the play, and the final encounter at Bosworth Field sees the king unhorsed, crying those famous words: "A horse! A horse! My kingdom for a horse!"

In a dramatic encounter, Richard's cousin, Henry Tudor, kills Richard and thus ascends the throne in his place. The marriage of Henry to Elizabeth of York, the very girl that Richard was trying to marry after killing his wife, is where we get the Tudor rose: the red of Henry's Lancastrian line combined with Elizabeth's Yorkist heritage, and the wars between the two roses is now over.

---

5. In the oldest-known published version of the play, it's called the The Tragedy of King Richard the Third, but being part of the First Tetralogy of a history cycle of plays, I've kept its classification as a History play.

SELECTIONS FROM RICHARD III

COPYWORK 1

GLOUCESTER

Now is the winter of our discontent

Made glorious summer by this sun of York;

And all the clouds that lour'd upon our house

In the deep bosom of the ocean buried.

Now are our brows bound with victorious wreaths;

Our bruised arms hung up for monuments;

Our stern alarums changed to merry meetings,

Our dreadful marches to delightful measures.

Grim-visaged war hath smooth'd his wrinkled front;

And now, instead of mounting barded steeds

To fright the souls of fearful adversaries,

He capers nimbly in a lady's chamber

To the lascivious pleasing of a lute.

But I, that am not shaped for sportive tricks,

Nor made to court an amorous looking-glass;

I, that am rudely stamp'd, and want love's majesty

To strut before a wanton ambling nymph;

I, that am curtail'd of this fair proportion,

Cheated of feature by dissembling nature,

Deformed, unfinish'd, sent before my time

Into this breathing world, scarce half made up,

And that so lamely and unfashionable

That dogs bark at me as I halt by them;

Why, I, in this weak piping time of peace,

Have no delight to pass away the time,

Unless to spy my shadow in the sun

And descant on mine own deformity:

And therefore, since I cannot prove a lover,

To entertain these fair well-spoken days,

I am determined to prove a villain

And hate the idle pleasures of these days.

Plots have I laid, inductions dangerous,

By drunken prophecies, libels and dreams,

To set my brother Clarence and the king

In deadly hate the one against the other:

And if King Edward be as true and just

As I am subtle, false and treacherous,

This day should Clarence closely be mew'd up,

About a prophecy, which says that 'G'

Of Edward's heirs the murderer shall be.

Dive, thoughts, down to my soul: here

Clarence comes. (I.i.1-42)

Richard's first soliloquy opens the play, and establishes our villain from the outset. It's not so much a problem that, as he says, he's not suited to the time of peace, but the way he uses a deformity in his body to justify villainy, the first order of which is to turn his brother, Edward, against his brother Clarence.

As is usual in Shakespeare, there are metahpors that help us with his meaning. If you don't look too carefully, the first line might look as though Richard is unhappy because we start in the "winter of our discontent," but make sure you always persist to the end of his sentences before trying to tease out the meaning of them.

Now is the winter of our discontent

Made glorious summer by this sun of York;

Shakespeare isn't saying that Richard is discontented and wintry, but quite the opposite: if it's the wintertime of our unhappiness, then it's like a double negative. The period during which we were unhappy is now at an end, and the cause is the sunny warmth of summer brought by the House of York, or more specifically, the SON of York, that is, Edward IV. By conquering Henry VI and being re-crowned, Edward is bringing peace to to the realm after decades of civil war.

Toward the end of this speech, notice the prophecy that Richard refers to, where it has been said that "G" is going to bring an end to Edward's reign. We later hear from Richard's brother, the Duke of Clarence, that Edward is rather superstitious about a lot of dreams and prophecies, so when a wizard warns Edward about someone whose name begins with "G", Clarence is worried that Edward will think it's him because his first name is George.

Of course we, the audience, know that it will be Richard, the Duke of Gloucester - "G" for Gloucester.

SELECTIONS FROM RICHARD III

COPYWORK 2

GLOUCESTER

What news abroad?

HASTINGS

No news so bad abroad as this at home;
The King is sickly, weak and melancholy,
And his physicians fear him mightily.

GLOUCESTER

Now, by Saint Paul, this news is bad indeed.
O, he hath kept an evil diet long,
And overmuch consumed his royal person:
'Tis very grievous to be thought upon.
What, is he in his bed?

HASTINGS

He is.

GLOUCESTER

Go you before, and I will follow you.

Exit HASTINGS

He cannot live, I hope; and must not die

Till George be pack'd with post-horse up to heaven.

I'll in, to urge his hatred more to Clarence,

With lies well steel'd with weighty arguments;

And, if I fall not in my deep intent,

Clarence hath not another day to live:

Which done, God take King Edward to his mercy,

And leave the world for me to bustle in!

For then I'll marry Warwick's youngest daughter.

What though I kill'd her husband and her father?

The readiest way to make the wench amends

Is to become her husband and her father:

The which will I; not all so much for love

As for another secret close intent,

By marrying her which I must reach unto.

But yet I run before my horse to market:

Clarence still breathes; Edward still lives and reigns:

When they are gone, then must I count my gains.
(I.i.135-165)

∾

We learn now that Edward IV is actualy unwell. In Richard's soliloquy, we see that he needs Edward to stay alive long enough for Richard to despatch Clarence, then it will be fine for Edward to die, he says, and let Richard "bustle in," presumably to the throne as king or at least protector, ruling on behalf of Edward's young son. The next part of his plan is to marry "Warwick's daughter" - this was Lady Anne Neville, and an outrageous conquest considering that she was the widow of Henry VI's son, the Lancastrian Prince Edward whom, in Shakespeare's version at least, Richard killed on the battlefield before the timeline of this play. The curious phrase on line 161 - "for another secret close intent" - has baffled scholars: what is this secret plan that Richard refers to? We never find out for sure. Possibly, he just means his plan to become king, but it could also just be Shakespeare's way of showing how secretive and scheming Richard is, in that he has other secret plans in mind.

SELECTIONS FROM RICHARD III

COPYWORK 3

LADY ANNE

Set down, set down your honourable load,

If honour may be shrouded in a hearse,

Whilst I awhile obsequiously lament

The untimely fall of virtuous Lancaster.

Poor key-cold figure of a holy king!

Pale ashes of the house of Lancaster!

Thou bloodless remnant of that royal blood!

Be it lawful that I invocate thy ghost,

To hear the lamentations of Poor Anne,

Wife to thy Edward, to thy slaughter'd son,

Stabb'd by the selfsame hand that made these wounds!

Lo, in these windows that let forth thy life,

I pour the helpless balm of my poor eyes.

Cursed be the hand that made these fatal holes!

Cursed be the heart that had the heart to do it!

Cursed the blood that let this blood from hence!

More direful hap betide that hated wretch,

That makes us wretched by the death of thee,

Than I can wish to adders, spiders, toads,

Or any creeping venom'd thing that lives!

If ever he have child, abortive be it,

Prodigious, and untimely brought to light,

Whose ugly and unnatural aspect

May fright the hopeful mother at the view;

And that be heir to his unhappiness!

If ever he have wife, let her he made

A miserable by the death of him

As I am made by my poor lord and thee!

Come, now towards Chertsey with your holy load,

Taken from Paul's to be interred there;

And still, as you are weary of the weight,

Rest you, whiles I lament King Henry's corse. (I.ii.1-33)

Enter GLOUCESTER

～

In the very next scene that follows the nasty Richard soliloquy, we meet "Warwick's daughter", Lady Anne. The whole speech is full of irony since, as she laments the corpse of Henry VI on its way to burial, we know that her venom and curses are raining down on the man who has designs to marry her. How unfortunate, then, to say: "If ever he have a wife, let her he made a miserable by the death of him as I am made by my poor lord and thee!" In other words, may the murderer's wife be as miserable at his death as she, that is Anne, is being made by the deaths of her lord (husband) Prince Edward and Henry ... in the end, it turns out she has just been cursing herself!

You see, that's the thing about history plays. Nothing in them is a mystery: everyone who watches the play should know that Lady Anne DID marry Richard of Gloucester, and thus, all of her protests and curses are undermined in the audience's eyes.

An example of dramatic irony. We, the audience, know the full significance of her words, even if she doesn't.

Finally, notice in line 31 when Anne says that Henry is "taken from Paul's". She is remarking that Henry's loss of the crown means that he is no longer due a royal burial at St Paul's Cathedral, but is instead, bound for the lesser resting place of Chertsey Abbey, about 30 miles southwest of London.

SELECTIONS FROM RICHARD III

COPYWORK 4

GLOUCESTER (...)

Teach not thy lips such scorn, for they were made

For kissing, lady, not for such contempt.

If thy revengeful heart cannot forgive,

Lo, here I lend thee this sharp-pointed sword;

Which if thou please to hide in this true bosom.

And let the soul forth that adoreth thee,

I lay it naked to the deadly stroke,

And humbly beg the death upon my knee.

He lays his breast open: she offers at it with his sword

Nay, do not pause; for I did kill King Henry,

But 'twas thy beauty that provoked me.

Nay, now dispatch; 'twas I that stabb'd young Edward,

But 'twas thy heavenly face that set me on.

Here she lets fall the sword

Take up the sword again, or take up me.

LADY ANNE
Arise, dissembler: though I wish thy death,
I will not be the executioner.

GLOUCESTER
Then bid me kill myself, and I will do it.

LADY ANNE
I have already.

GLOUCESTER
Tush, that was in thy rage:
Speak it again, and, even with the word,
That hand, which, for thy love, did kill thy love,
Shall, for thy love, kill a far truer love;
To both their deaths thou shalt be accessary.

LADY ANNE
I would I knew thy heart. (I.ii.173-194)

∽

We pick up Richard's wooing of Lady Anne in mid-scene. Much of what has come before is Anne's reproofs and curses, while Richard moons about with false claims that his hatred of Prince Edward was due to jealousy of her beauty. He dares her to kill him with a sword, even goading her by admitting he killed Henry and Edward. She drops the sword, which spurs on Richard to go a step further - kill him or marry him, or if she do neither, he threatens to kill himself. When she utters the final line here, "I would I knew thy heart," Richard has won.

SELECTIONS FROM RICHARD III

COPYWORK 5

GLOUCESTER (...)

Was ever woman in this humour woo'd?

Was ever woman in this humour won?

I'll have her; but I will not keep her long.

What! I, that kill'd her husband and his father,

To take her in her heart's extremest hate,

With curses in her mouth, tears in her eyes,

The bleeding witness of her hatred by;

Having God, her conscience, and these bars

against me,

And I nothing to back my suit at all,

But the plain devil and dissembling looks,

And yet to win her, all the world to nothing!

Ha!

Hath she forgot already that brave prince,

Edward, her lord, whom I, some three months since,

Stabb'd in my angry mood at Tewksbury?

A sweeter and a lovelier gentleman,

Framed in the prodigality of nature,

Young, valiant, wise, and, no doubt, right royal,

The spacious world cannot again afford

And will she yet debase her eyes on me,

That cropp'd the golden prime of this sweet prince,

And made her widow to a woful bed?

On me, whose all not equals Edward's moiety?

On me, that halt and am unshapen thus?

My dukedom to a beggarly denier,

I do mistake my person all this while:

Upon my life, she finds, although I cannot,

Myself to be a marvellous proper man.

I'll be at charges for a looking-glass,

And entertain some score or two of tailors,

To study fashions to adorn my body:

Since I am crept in favour with myself,

Will maintain it with some little cost.

But first I'll turn yon fellow in his grave;

And then return lamenting to my love.

Shine out, fair sun, till I have bought a glass,

That I may see my shadow as I pass. (I.ii.229-265)

Exit

❧

A famous soliloquy - "can you believe how persuasive I am?!" She won't last.

SELECTIONS FROM RICHARD III

COPYWORK 6

QUEEN ELIZABETH

Brother of Gloucester, you mistake the matter.

The king, of his own royal disposition,

And not provoked by any suitor else;

Aiming, belike, at your interior hatred,

Which in your outward actions shows itself

Against my kindred, brothers, and myself,

Makes him to send; that thereby he may gather

The ground of your ill-will, and so remove it.

GLOUCESTER

I cannot tell: the world is grown so bad,

That wrens make prey where eagles dare not perch:

Since every Jack became a gentleman

There's many a gentle person made a Jack.

QUEEN ELIZABETH

Come, come, we know your meaning, brother

Gloucester;

You envy my advancement and my friends':

God grant we never may have need of you!

GLOUCESTER

Meantime, God grants that we have need of you:

Your brother is imprison'd by your means,

Myself disgraced, and the nobility

Held in contempt; whilst many fair promotions

Are daily given to ennoble those

That scarce, some two days since, were worth a noble.

QUEEN ELIZABETH

By Him that raised me to this careful height

From that contented hap which I enjoy'd,

I never did incense his majesty

Against the Duke of Clarence, but have been

An earnest advocate to plead for him.

My lord, you do me shameful injury,

Falsely to draw me in these vile suspects. (I.iii.62-88)

~

In this scene, we're introduced to King Edward's wife, Elizabeth. She was of middle-ranking aristocracy and a widow when Edward married her, a union that caused consternation amongst Edward's biggest supporters. You can see in this scene how Richard views Elizabeth and her family as upstarts, and insinuates that they're plotting against him and Clarence. Always playing the victim, our Richard.

RICHARD, DUKE OF GLOUCESTER

Have done thy charm, thou hateful with'red hag.

QUEEN MARGARET

And leave out thee? Stay, dog, for thou shalt hear me.

If heaven have any grievous plague in store

Exceeding those that I can wish upon thee,

O, let them keep it till thy sins be ripe,

And then hurl down their indignation

On thee, the troubler of the poor world's peace!

The worm of conscience still begnaw thy soul!

Thy friends suspect for traitors while thou liv'st,

And take deep traitors for thy dearest friends!

No sleep close up that deadly eye of thine,

Unless it be while some tormenting dream

Affrights thee with a hell of ugly devils!

Thou elvish-mark'd, abortive, rooting hog!

Thou that wast seal'd in thy nativity

The slave of nature and the son of hell!

Thou slander of thy heavy mother's womb!

Thou loathed issue of thy father's loins!

Thou rag of honor! Thou detested—

RICHARD, DUKE OF GLOUCESTER

Margaret.

QUEEN MARGARET

Richard!

RICHARD, DUKE OF GLOUCESTER

Ha! (I.iii.214-232)

∾

Into the vipers' nest of unhappy, feuding courtiers comes the widow of Henry VI, Margaret. She has just been hurling curses upon all those present, and here in our selection, turns her venom onto Richard. She can hardly throw enough horrid epithets at him. She prophesies that he will be unable to tell who is friend or foe. Next, she hits at his ability to sleep (a curse which is later repeated in <u>Macbeth</u>). Richard puts an end to her ranting by finishing her sentence with her name, thus meaning that Margaret is detested rather than Richard. The company has a good joke over that at her expense, but she is not daunted. She knows that they have usurped her position, and foreshadows that each will pay dearly for it.

SELECTIONS FROM RICHARD III

COPYWORK 8

RICHARD, DUKE OF GLOUCESTER

I do the wrong, and first begin to brawl.

The secret mischiefs that I set abroach

I lay unto the grievous charge of others.

Clarence, who I indeed have cast in darkness,

I do beweep to many simple gulls—

Namely, to Derby, Hastings, Buckingham—

And tell them 'tis the Queen and her allies

That stir the King against the Duke my brother.

Now they believe it, and withal whet me

To be reveng'd on Rivers, Dorset, Grey.

But then I sigh, and, with a piece of scripture,

Tell them that God bids us do good for evil:

And thus I clothe my naked villainy

With odd old ends stol'n forth of holy writ,

And seem a saint, when most I play the devil.

ENTER TWO MURDERERS.

But soft, here come my executioners. (I.iii.323-338)

Richard practically hugs himself with success at stirring up trouble. He says the he's the one causing all the trouble ("do the wrong"), but that he is the first to pick a fight with someone else, blaming them for the mean things as a way of deflecting the real prime mover behind them.

SELECTIONS FROM RICHARD III

COPYWORK 9

CLARENCE

Methoughts that I had broken from the Tower,

And was embark'd to cross to Burgundy;

And, in my company, my brother Gloucester;

Who from my cabin tempted me to walk

Upon the hatches: thence we looked toward England,

And cited up a thousand fearful times,

During the wars of York and Lancaster

That had befall'n us. As we paced along

Upon the giddy footing of the hatches,

Methought that Gloucester stumbled; and, in falling,

Struck me, that thought to stay him, overboard,

Into the tumbling billows of the main.

Lord, Lord! methought, what pain it was to drown!

What dreadful noise of waters in mine ears!

What ugly sights of death within mine eyes!

Methought I saw a thousand fearful wrecks;

Ten thousand men that fishes gnaw'd upon;

Wedges of gold, great anchors, heaps of pearl,

Inestimable stones, unvalued jewels,

All scatter'd in the bottom of the sea:

Some lay in dead men's skulls; and, in those holes

Where eyes did once inhabit, there were crept,

As 'twere in scorn of eyes, reflecting gems,

Which woo'd the slimy bottom of the deep,

And mock'd the dead bones that lay scatter'd by. (I.iv.9-34)

By the time we pop in to see what Clarence is up to in the Tower, we know that he's doomed. After all, just a few lines before in scene 3, Richard has employed two murderers for the purpose. Clarence's fate is further underlined when we hear about his dream, that Richard basically pushes him off a ship and he drowns. Now here's an interesting tidbit: most people think it's historical fact that Clarence was executed by drowning in a vat of wine, but the truth is, we have come to believe this mode of death because Shakespeare wrote it here in his play. In real life, there's a lot of mystery surrounding the end of Clarence. We do know that Richard didn't do it, but that it was Edward, and we know that it was because Clarence was plotting against his brother, the king. But drowning in malmsey? That seems to be Shakespearean whimsy.

SELECTIONS FROM RICHARD III

COPYWORK 10

Enter QUEEN ELIZABETH, with her hair about her ears; RIVERS, and DORSET after her

QUEEN ELIZABETH

Oh, who shall hinder me to wail and weep,

To chide my fortune, and torment myself?

I'll join with black despair against my soul,

And to myself become an enemy.

DUCHESS OF YORK

What means this scene of rude impatience?

QUEEN ELIZABETH

To make an act of tragic violence:

Edward, my lord, your son, our king, is dead.

Why grow the branches now the root is wither'd?

Why wither not the leaves the sap being gone?

If you will live, lament; if die, be brief,

That our swift-winged souls may catch the king's;

Or, like obedient subjects, follow him

To his new kingdom of perpetual rest.

DUCHESS OF YORK

Ah, so much interest have I in thy sorrow

As I had title in thy noble husband!

I have bewept a worthy husband's death,

And lived by looking on his images:

But now two mirrors of his princely semblance

Are crack'd in pieces by malignant death,

And I for comfort have but one false glass,

Which grieves me when I see my shame in him.

Thou art a widow; yet thou art a mother,

And hast the comfort of thy children left thee:

But death hath snatch'd my husband from mine arms,

And pluck'd two crutches from my feeble limbs,

Edward and Clarence. O, what cause have I,

Thine being but a moiety of my grief,

To overgo thy plaints and drown thy cries! (II.ii.35-62)

∽

The queen, Elizabeth, comes into the room with her hair unkempt, a sign of grief and distraction. We know from the previous scene that Edward has died, but his mother, the Duchess of York, isn't aware of the news. Instead, she has just been fending off questions from Clarence's children, trying to hide the truth of his death from them. Elizabeth has come to bring news of Edward's. The Duchess responds by saying how she knows tragedy, too: her husband, Richard of York, was killed in battle, and as she says, she is reminded of him every day by the offspring that look like him. However, now that Edward and Clarence are both dead, two of the mirrors that reflected her husband's face have cracked. The third, Richard, she called "one false glass" - a fake or misshapen mirror - and looking on him makes her grieve and feel shame. Her final words here are to chastise Elizabeth - she lost both husband and sons, and her grief is the more.

SELECTIONS FROM RICHARD III

COPYWORK 11

THIRD CITIZEN

Doth this news hold of good King Edward's death?

SECOND CITIZEN

Ay, sir, it is too true; God help the while!

THIRD CITIZEN

Then, masters, look to see a troublous world.

FIRST CITIZEN

No, no; by God's good grace his son shall reign.

THIRD CITIZEN

Woe to the land that's govern'd by a child!

SECOND CITIZEN

In him there is a hope of government,

That in his nonage council under him,

And in his full and ripen'd years himself,

No doubt, shall then and till then govern well.

FIRST CITIZEN

So stood the state when Henry the Sixth

Was crown'd in Paris but at nine months old.

THIRD CITIZEN

Stood the state so? No, no, good friends, God wot;

For then this land was famously enrich'd

With politic grave counsel; then the king

Had virtuous uncles to protect his grace.

FIRST CITIZEN

Why, so hath this, both by the father and mother.

THIRD CITIZEN

Better it were they all came by the father,

Or by the father there were none at all;

For emulation now, who shall be nearest,

Will touch us all too near, if God prevent not.

O, full of danger is the Duke of Gloucester!

And the queen's sons and brothers haught and proud:

And were they to be ruled, and not to rule,

This sickly land might solace as before.

FIRST CITIZEN

Come, come, we fear the worst; all shall be well.

THIRD CITIZEN

When clouds appear, wise men put on their cloaks;

When great leaves fall, the winter is at hand;

When the sun sets, who doth not look for night?

Untimely storms make men expect a dearth.

All may be well; but, if God sort it so,

'Tis more than we deserve, or I expect. (II.iii.11-41)

⚬

Here is a type of scene that's often seen in Shakespeare - a scene I like to call the "bystanders' view of the world" or "testing the way the wind blows" scene. Basically, these are scenes of super-minor characters who summarize the situation at this point in the play. In this case, we have three citizens who discuss how Edward has died and his young son is due to be crowned, but how either Richard or Rivers will be acting ruler. The Third Citizen is particularly cynical about this, saying the one is dangerous and the other, an upstart. Notice the references to nature. The inevitable result of this situation, like the negative signs of rain, winter, night, and famine, does not bode well for the country's future. Nor for Rivers, for who could stand in the way of Richard's plans to be in charge?

SELECTIONS FROM RICHARD III

COPYWORK 12

GLOUCESTER

Go, after, after, cousin Buckingham.

The mayor towards Guildhall hies him in all post:

There, at your meet'st advantage of the time,

Infer the bastardy of Edward's children:

Tell them how Edward put to death a citizen,

Only for saying he would make his son

Heir to the crown; meaning indeed his house,

Which, by the sign thereof was termed so.

Moreover, urge his hateful luxury

And bestial appetite in change of lust;

Which stretched to their servants, daughters, wives,

Even where his lustful eye or savage heart,

Without control, listed to make his prey.

Nay, for a need, thus far come near my person:

Tell them, when that my mother went with child

Of that unsatiate Edward, noble York

My princely father then had wars in France

And, by just computation of the time,

Found that the issue was not his begot;

Which well appeared in his lineaments,

Being nothing like the noble duke my father:

But touch this sparingly, as 'twere far off,

Because you know, my lord, my mother lives. (III.v.73-96)

By the time we get to this point in the play, Richard has dispatched so many people that we can hardly keep up with the body count. He has sent Rivers, Elizabeth's brother, to Pomfret Castle for execution, the very same castle where King Richard II is killed in that other history play. Next, he beheads a nobleman named Hastings for supposed conspiracy with a witch who, Richard says, caused his arm to wither. Now for his next series of tricks: cast aspersions on the character of the dead king. First, spread a rumor that Edward's sons are bastards (historically, it's believed that Edward was betrothed to at least one other woman before marrying Elizabeth: engagements like this took precedence over his relationship with Elizabeth and thus voided his marriage to her). Next, remind the citizens how Edward executed a man just because he'd named his public house "The Crown" and told his son he'd inherit the crown some day, arguing that doing so was tantamount to claiming the throne for himself. Finally, cast doubt on Edward's own legitimacy: not only was he conceived while his father was fighting in France, so Richard says, but he doesn't look anything like his dad. "Go gently," Richard tells his co-conspirator, Buckingham. "Just hint at this ever so slightly since my mother is still alive."

SELECTIONS FROM RICHARD III

COPYWORK 13

QUEEN ELIZABETH

Kind sister, thanks: we'll enter all together.

Enter BRAKENBURY

And, in good time, here the lieutenant comes.

Master lieutenant, pray you, by your leave,

How doth the prince, and my young son of York?

BRAKENBURY

Right well, dear madam. By your patience,

I may not suffer you to visit them;

The king hath straitly charged the contrary.

QUEEN ELIZABETH

The king! why, who's that?

BRAKENBURY

I cry you mercy: I mean the lord protector.

QUEEN ELIZABETH

The Lord protect him from that kingly title!

Hath he set bounds betwixt their love and me?

I am their mother; who should keep me from them?

DUCHESS OF YORK

I am their fathers mother; I will see them.

LADY ANNE

Their aunt I am in law, in love their mother:

Then bring me to their sights; I'll bear thy blame

And take thy office from thee, on my peril.

BRAKENBURY

No, madam, no; I may not leave it so:

I am bound by oath, and therefore pardon me.

Exit

Enter LORD STANLEY

LORD STANLEY

Let me but meet you, ladies, one hour hence,

And I'll salute your grace of York as mother,

And reverend looker on, of two fair queens.

To LADY ANNE

Come, madam, you must straight to Westminster,

There to be crowned Richard's royal queen.

QUEEN ELIZABETH

O, cut my lace in sunder, that my pent heart

May have some scope to beat, or else I swoon

With this dead-killing news!

LADY ANNE

Despiteful tidings! O unpleasing news! (IV.i.12-39)

≈

The three main women of the play, Queen Elizabeth (Edward's widow), the Duchess of York (Edward and Richard's mother), and Lady Anne (Richard's wife) arrive at the Tower to see the young princes, Edward and Richard, the late-king Edward's sons. They are turned away by the Lieutenant of the Tower, Brakenbury, who lets slip that Richard is calling himself king now. Lord Stanley enters to call the women to Westminster for the coronation. Elizabeth is mortified, and so is Anne. By the by, Lord Stanley is the step-father of a character called Richmond, a courtier currently in France and a key to the denoument of the play: he's also known as Henry Tudor, the victor over Richard III and thereby the next king, Henry VII.

SELECTIONS FROM RICHARD III

COPYWORK 14

KING RICHARD III

O bitter consequence,

That Edward still should live! 'True, noble prince!'

Cousin, thou wert not wont to be so dull:

Shall I be plain? I wish the bastards dead;

And I would have it suddenly perform'd.

What sayest thou? speak suddenly; be brief.

BUCKINGHAM

Your grace may do your pleasure.

KING RICHARD III

Tut, tut, thou art all ice, thy kindness freezeth:

Say, have I thy consent that they shall die?

BUCKINGHAM

Give me some breath, some little pause, my lord

Before I positively herein:

I will resolve your grace immediately.

Exit

CATESBY

[Aside to a stander by]

The king is angry: see, he bites the lip.

KING RICHARD III

I will converse with iron-witted fools

And unrespective boys: none are for me

That look into me with considerate eyes:

High-reaching Buckingham grows circumspect.

Boy!

PAGE

My lord?

KING RICHARD III

Know'st thou not any whom corrupting gold

Would tempt unto a close exploit of death?

PAGE

My lord, I know a discontented gentleman,

Whose humble means match not his haughty mind:

Gold were as good as twenty orators,

And will, no doubt, tempt him to any thing.

KING RICHARD III

What is his name?

PAGE

His name, my lord, is Tyrrel.

KING RICHARD III

I partly know the man: go, call him hither.

Exit PAGE

The deep-revolving witty Buckingham

No more shall be the neighbour to my counsel:

Hath he so long held out with me untired,

And stops he now for breath?

Enter STANLEY

How now! what news with you?

STANLEY

My lord, I hear the Marquis Dorset's fled

To Richmond, in those parts beyond the sea

Where he abides.

Stands apart

KING RICHARD III

Catesby!

CATESBY

My lord?

KING RICHARD III

Rumour it abroad

That Anne, my wife, is sick and like to die:

I will take order for her keeping close.

Inquire me out some mean-born gentleman,

Whom I will marry straight to Clarence' daughter:

The boy is foolish, and I fear not him.

Look, how thou dream'st! I say again, give out

That Anne my wife is sick and like to die:

About it; for it stands me much upon,

To stop all hopes whose growth may damage me.

Exit CATESBY

I must be married to my brother's daughter,

Or else my kingdom stands on brittle glass.

Murder her brothers, and then marry her!

Uncertain way of gain! But I am in

So far in blood that sin will pluck on sin:

Tear-falling pity dwells not in this eye. (IV.ii.16-69)

~

This interchange is hyuuuge! In the space of a few lines, Richard heaps rash decision upon rash decision. First, he falls out with his closest advisor, Buckingham, because Richard wants the young prince executed but Buckingham is reluctant. "No more shall he be a neighbor to my counsel," Richard says, deciding there and then to break his ties with him. We, as the audience, suspect that Buckingham's days are numbered.

Next, Richard ferrets out someone dastardly and disaffected enough to murder the princes in the Tower. This is a man identified as Tyrrel.

Then we hear about Richmond: Elizabeth's son, the Marquis of Dorset (a son from her first marriage), has fled to join Richmond and his forces in France. This is foreshadowing, but also seems to push Richard to desperate measures.

Suddenly, he tells Catesby that Anne, his wife, is sick. "Sick" with inverted commas. Richard will make sure that she is so "sick" that she dies, thus making way for him to marry someone else. That someone else, he decides, will be Edward's daughter, the young Princess Elizabeth. (She later marries Richmond, and it's her white rose of York and Richmond's red rose of Lancaster that combine to form the Tudor rose).

In a line that is reminiscent of Macbeth, Richard muses: "I am in so far in blood that sin will pluck on sin." In other words, I've gone so far in murdering everyone that sin must beget more sin - it's inevitable.

Royalty free image from Pixabay

SELECTIONS FROM RICHARD III

COPYWORK 15

TYRREL

The tyrannous and bloody deed is done.

The most arch of piteous massacre

That ever yet this land was guilty of.

Dighton and Forrest, whom I did suborn

To do this ruthless piece of butchery,

Although they were flesh'd villains, bloody dogs,

Melting with tenderness and kind compassion

Wept like two children in their deaths' sad stories.

'Lo, thus' quoth Dighton, 'lay those tender babes:'

'Thus, thus,' quoth Forrest, 'girdling one another

Within their innocent alabaster arms:

Their lips were four red roses on a stalk,

Which in their summer beauty kiss'd each other.

A book of prayers on their pillow lay;

Which once,' quoth Forrest, 'almost changed my mind;

But O! the devil'—there the villain stopp'd

Whilst Dighton thus told on: 'We smothered

The most replenished sweet work of nature,

That from the prime creation e'er she framed.'

Thus both are gone with conscience and remorse;

They could not speak; and so I left them both,

To bring this tidings to the bloody king.

And here he comes. (IV.iii.1-23)

≈

This is a description of perhaps one of the most famous murders in history - murders that may or may not have happened, as no one knows for sure. Tyrrel, at Richard's behest, arranges for the young princes in the Tower to be "dispatched". His hard-bitten henchman, Dighton and Forrest, are brought to tears as they recount how they ended the peaceful slumber of the two young brothers.

SELECTIONS FROM RICHARD III

COPYWORK 16

DUCHESS OF YORK

Blind sight, dead life, poor mortal living ghost,

Woe's scene, world's shame, grave's due by life usurp'd,

Brief abstract and record of tedious days,

Rest thy unrest on England's lawful earth,

Sitting down

Unlawfully made drunk with innocents' blood!

QUEEN ELIZABETH

O, that thou wouldst as well afford a grave

As thou canst yield a melancholy seat!

Then would I hide my bones, not rest them here.

O, who hath any cause to mourn but I?

Sitting down by her

QUEEN MARGARET

If ancient sorrow be most reverend,

Give mine the benefit of seniory,

And let my woes frown on the upper hand.

If sorrow can admit society,

Sitting down with them

Tell o'er your woes again by viewing mine:

I had an Edward, till a Richard kill'd him;

I had a Harry, till a Richard kill'd him:

Thou hadst an Edward, till a Richard kill'd him;

Thou hadst a Richard, till a Richard killed him;

DUCHESS OF YORK

I had a Richard too, and thou didst kill him;

I had a Rutland too, thou holp'st to kill him.

QUEEN MARGARET

Thou hadst a Clarence too, and Richard kill'd him.

From forth the kennel of thy womb hath crept

A hell-hound that doth hunt us all to death:

That dog, that had his teeth before his eyes,

To worry lambs and lap their gentle blood,

That foul defacer of God's handiwork,

That excellent grand tyrant of the earth,

That reigns in galled eyes of weeping souls,

Thy womb let loose, to chase us to our graves.

O upright, just, and true-disposing God,

How do I thank thee, that this carnal cur

Preys on the issue of his mother's body,

And makes her pew-fellow with others' moan!

DUCHESS OF YORK

O Harry's wife, triumph not in my woes!

God witness with me, I have wept for thine. (IV.iv.29-62)

✑

The three widows grieve a catalogue of deaths: the real "glory" of the Wars of the Roses. There are two things I find touching here. The first is, although Margaret is an enemy to the house of York, being the queen of the dead Lancastrian King Henry, she is still drawn to sit down with the York widows to share a dialogue of lamentation. With tensions running high, she lists all the victims of the Duchess's son, Richard, gloating that it's just desserts for the York's to be vicitms of him, too. Then the Duchess protests: Don't gloat, she says. I honestly have shed tears for your misfortune in the past. This is the second thing I find touching. Feuding families can still keenly feel the losses on the other side.

SELECTIONS FROM RICHARD III

COPYWORK 17

KING RICHARD III

As I intend to prosper and repent,

So thrive I in my dangerous attempt

Of hostile arms! myself myself confound!

Heaven and fortune bar me happy hours!

Day, yield me not thy light; nor, night, thy rest!

Be opposite all planets of good luck

To my proceedings, if, with pure heart's love,

Immaculate devotion, holy thoughts,

I tender not thy beauteous princely daughter!

In her consists my happiness and thine;

Without her, follows to this land and me,

To thee, herself, and many a Christian soul,

Death, desolation, ruin and decay:

It cannot be avoided but by this;

It will not be avoided but by this.

Therefore, good mother,—I must can you so—

Be the attorney of my love to her:

Plead what I will be, not what I have been;

Not my deserts, but what I will deserve:

Urge the necessity and state of times,

And be not peevish-fond in great designs.

QUEEN ELIZABETH

Shall I be tempted of the devil thus?

KING RICHARD III

Ay, if the devil tempt thee to do good.

QUEEN ELIZABETH

Shall I forget myself to be myself?

KING RICHARD III

Ay, if yourself's remembrance wrong yourself.

QUEEN ELIZABETH

But thou didst kill my children.

KING RICHARD III

But in your daughter's womb I bury them:

Where in that nest of spicery they shall breed

Selves of themselves, to your recomforture.

QUEEN ELIZABETH

Shall I go win my daughter to thy will?

KING RICHARD III

And be a happy mother by the deed.

QUEEN ELIZABETH

I go. Write to me very shortly.

And you shall understand from me her mind.

KING RICHARD III

Bear her my true love's kiss; and so, farewell.

Exit QUEEN ELIZABETH

Relenting fool, and shallow, changing woman!
(IV.iv.420-454)

∼

In the very same scene of the widows' lament, Richard convinces Elizabeth that he really loves her daughter and wants to marry her. How he does this is through the most incredible verbal gymnastics: basically he says, if I did kill your sons then I'm sorry about that, but I'll create new sons by marrying your daughter. Ew. As Elizabeth leaves to break the news, Richard's smile disappears. Fool, he says. But she is no fool! We find out later that she arranges a match with the rebel Richmond instead.

SELECTIONS FROM RICHARD III

COPYWORK 18 AND 19

Ghost of PRINCE EDWARD
[To KING RICHARD III]
Let me sit heavy on thy soul to-morrow!
Think, how thou stab'dst me in my prime of youth
At Tewksbury: despair, therefore, and die!

To RICHMOND
Be cheerful, Richmond; for the wronged souls
Of butcher'd princes fight in thy behalf
King Henry's issue, Richmond, comforts thee.
Enter the Ghost of King Henry VI

Ghost of KING HENRY VI
[To KING RICHARD III]
When I was mortal, my anointed body
By thee was punched full of deadly holes

Think on the Tower and me: despair, and die!

Harry the Sixth bids thee despair, and die!

To RICHMOND

Virtuous and holy, be thou conqueror!

Harry, that prophesied thou shouldst be king,

Doth comfort thee in thy sleep: live, and flourish!

Enter the Ghost of CLARENCE

Ghost of CLARENCE

[To KING RICHARD III]

Let me sit heavy on thy soul to-morrow!

I, that was wash'd to death with fulsome wine,

Poor Clarence, by thy guile betrayed to death!

To-morrow in the battle think on me,

And fall thy edgeless sword: despair, and die!—

To RICHMOND

Thou offspring of the house of Lancaster

The wronged heirs of York do pray for thee

Good angels guard thy battle! live, and flourish!

Enter the Ghosts of RIVERS, GRAY, and VAUGHAN

Ghost of RIVERS

[To KING RICHARD III]

Let me sit heavy on thy soul to-morrow,

Rivers. that died at Pomfret! despair, and die!

Ghost of GREY

[To KING RICHARD III]

Think upon Grey, and let thy soul despair!

Ghost of VAUGHAN

[To KING RICHARD III]

Think upon Vaughan, and, with guilty fear,

Let fall thy lance: despair, and die!

ALL

[To RICHMOND]

Awake, and think our wrongs in Richard's bosom

Will conquer him! awake, and win the day! (V.iii.124-154)

(END Copywork 19)

(Begin Copywork 20)

Enter the Ghost of HASTINGS

Ghost of HASTINGS

[To KING RICHARD III]

Bloody and guilty, guiltily awake,

And in a bloody battle end thy days!

Think on Lord Hastings: despair, and die!

To RICHMOND

Quiet untroubled soul, awake, awake!

Arm, fight, and conquer, for fair England's sake!

Enter the Ghosts of the two young Princes

Ghosts of young Princes

[To KING RICHARD III]

Dream on thy cousins smother'd in the Tower:

Let us be led within thy bosom, Richard,

And weigh thee down to ruin, shame, and death!

Thy nephews' souls bid thee despair and die!

To RICHMOND

Sleep, Richmond, sleep in peace, and wake in joy;

Good angels guard thee from the boar's annoy!

Live, and beget a happy race of kings!

Edward's unhappy sons do bid thee flourish.

Enter the Ghost of LADY ANNE

Ghost of LADY ANNE

[To KING RICHARD III]

Richard, thy wife, that wretched Anne thy wife,

That never slept a quiet hour with thee,

Now fills thy sleep with perturbations

To-morrow in the battle think on me,

And fall thy edgeless sword: despair, and die!

To RICHMOND

Thou quiet soul, sleep thou a quiet sleep

Dream of success and happy victory!

Thy adversary's wife doth pray for thee.

Enter the Ghost of BUCKINGHAM

Ghost of BUCKINGHAM

[To KING RICHARD III]

The last was I that helped thee to the crown;

The last was I that felt thy tyranny:

O, in the battle think on Buckingham,

And die in terror of thy guiltiness!

Dream on, dream on, of bloody deeds and death:

Fainting, despair; despairing, yield thy breath!

To RICHMOND

I died for hope ere I could lend thee aid:

But cheer thy heart, and be thou not dismay'd:

God and good angel fight on Richmond's side;

And Richard falls in height of all his pride.

The Ghosts vanish

KING RICHARD III starts out of his dream (V.ii.155-188)

A pageant of ghosts visits Richard and Richmond in their respective tents as they sleep the night before the big battle. It's fairly self-explanatory about which man they're cheering for!

SELECTIONS FROM RICHARD III

COPYWORK 20

KING RICHARD III

Give me another horse: bind up my wounds.

Have mercy, Jesu!—Soft! I did but dream.

O coward conscience, how dost thou afflict me!

The lights burn blue. It is now dead midnight.

Cold fearful drops stand on my trembling flesh.

What do I fear? myself? there's none else by:

Richard loves Richard; that is, I am I.

Is there a murderer here? No. Yes, I am:

Then fly. What, from myself? Great reason why:

Lest I revenge. What, myself upon myself?

Alack. I love myself. Wherefore? for any good

That I myself have done unto myself?

O, no! alas, I rather hate myself

For hateful deeds committed by myself!

I am a villain: yet I lie. I am not.

Fool, of thyself speak well: fool, do not flatter.

My conscience hath a thousand several tongues,

And every tongue brings in a several tale,

And every tale condemns me for a villain.

Perjury, perjury, in the high'st degree

Murder, stem murder, in the direst degree;

All several sins, all used in each degree,

Throng to the bar, crying all, Guilty! guilty!

I shall despair. There is no creature loves me;

And if I die, no soul shall pity me:

Nay, wherefore should they, since that I myself

Find in myself no pity to myself?

Methought the souls of all that I had murder'd

Came to my tent; and every one did threat

To-morrow's vengeance on the head of Richard.

(V.iii.189-218)

~

Richard starts off this speech with a dream of battle then wakes himself up by shouting. He realises from the blueness of flames that it's very late - midnight. (Note also that blue flames were thought to indicate the presence of ghosts.) We then see a dual version of himself: he worries that a murderer might be in the tent with him, then admits that the murderer is himself. What follows are phrases, ideas, exclammations where he argues with himself and comes to two conclusions: yes, he is guilty. He is as guilty as being at the sentencing place in court, and this is an astonishing revelation after all his complacency about immoral behaviour. Second, he is isolated: no one will be sad should he die, including no pity from his very self. All this presages that the end is near for Richard, and even the start of this soliloquy where he asks for another horse is foreshadowing his ultimate and famous demise of being unhorsed on Bosworth Field.

SELECTIONS FROM RICHARD III

COPYWORK 21

KING RICHARD III

O Ratcliff, I have dream'd a fearful dream!

What thinkest thou, will our friends prove all true?

RATCLIFF

No doubt, my lord.

KING RICHARD III

O Ratcliff, I fear, I fear,—

RATCLIFF

Nay, good my lord, be not afraid of shadows.

KING RICHARD III

By the apostle Paul, shadows to-night

Have struck more terror to the soul of Richard

Than can the substance of ten thousand soldiers

Armed in proof, and led by shallow Richmond.

It is not yet near day. Come, go with me;

Under our tents I'll play the eaves-dropper,

To see if any mean to shrink from me.

Exeunt

Enter the Lords to RICHMOND, sitting in his tent

LORDS

Good morrow, Richmond!

RICHMOND

Cry mercy, lords and watchful gentlemen,

That you have ta'en a tardy sluggard here.

LORDS

How have you slept, my lord?

RICHMOND

The sweetest sleep, and fairest-boding dreams

That ever enter'd in a drowsy head,

Have I since your departure had, my lords.

Methought their souls, whose bodies Richard murder'd,

Came to my tent, and cried on victory:

I promise you, my soul is very jocund

In the remembrance of so fair a dream.

How far into the morning is it, lords? (V.iii.232-257)

~

I only include these lines here for you to see something clever that Shakespeare is doing: he's comparing the kinds of night these two - that is, Richard and Richmond - have just experienced. One has had a "fearful dream" with shadows that "have struck more terror" into Richard than a thousand soldiers would; the other has had "the sweetest sleep" where the souls of those who Richard had murdered came to him to cry "on victory", leaving his soul "very jocund" or happy and optimistic.

SELECTIONS FROM RICHARD III

COPYWORK 22

RICHMOND

Why, then 'tis time to arm and give direction.

His oration to his soldiers

More than I have said, loving countrymen,

The leisure and enforcement of the time

Forbids to dwell upon: yet remember this,

God and our good cause fight upon our side;

The prayers of holy saints and wronged souls,

Like high-rear'd bulwarks, stand before our faces;

Richard except, those whom we fight against

Had rather have us win than him they follow:

For what is he they follow? truly, gentlemen,

A bloody tyrant and a homicide;

One raised in blood, and one in blood establish'd;

One that made means to come by what he hath,

And slaughter'd those that were the means to help him;

Abase foul stone, made precious by the foil

Of England's chair, where he is falsely set;

One that hath ever been God's enemy:

Then, if you fight against God's enemy,

God will in justice ward you as his soldiers;

If you do sweat to put a tyrant down,

You sleep in peace, the tyrant being slain;

If you do fight against your country's foes,

Your country's fat shall pay your pains the hire;

If you do fight in safeguard of your wives,

Your wives shall welcome home the conquerors;

If you do free your children from the sword,

Your children's children quit it in your age.

Then, in the name of God and all these rights,

Advance your standards, draw your willing swords.

For me, the ransom of my bold attempt

Shall be this cold corpse on the earth's cold face;

But if I thrive, the gain of my attempt

The least of you shall share his part thereof.

Sound drums and trumpets boldly and cheerfully;

God   and   Saint   George!   Richmond   and   victory!
(V.iii.260-294)

~

On the brink of battle, Richmond reviews the situation: no one who fights for Richard is very happy about it because he's a "bloody tyrant and a homicide". Richmond then enumerates the justness of his cause with a series of "if ... then" statements, basically saying if you fight for the right cause, then you will be victorious. He invites his soldiers to draw their swords while he says his reward will be the "cold corpse" of Richard, and should Richmond win and become king, he will reward his followers. His last line that invokes Saint George reminds me of the end of Henry V's "Once more into the breach" speech: "God for Harry, England, and Saint George!", a play written by Shakespeare about six years after the one we're studying here.

SELECTIONS FROM RICHARD III

COPYWORK 23

KING RICHARD III

His oration to his Army

What shall I say more than I have inferr'd?

Remember whom you are to cope withal;

A sort of vagabonds, rascals, and runaways,

A scum of Bretons, and base lackey peasants,

Whom their o'er-cloyed country vomits forth

To desperate ventures and assured destruction.

You sleeping safe, they bring to you unrest;

You having lands, and blest with beauteous wives,

They would restrain the one, distain the other.

And who doth lead them but a paltry fellow,

Long kept in Bretagne at our mother's cost?

A milk-sop, one that never in his life

Felt so much cold as over shoes in snow?

Let's whip these stragglers o'er the seas again;

Lash hence these overweening rags of France,

These famish'd beggars, weary of their lives;

Who, but for dreaming on this fond exploit,

For want of means, poor rats, had hang'd themselves:

If we be conquer'd, let men conquer us,

And not these bastard Bretons; whom our fathers

Have in their own land beaten, bobb'd, and thump'd,

And in record, left them the heirs of shame.

Shall these enjoy our lands? lie with our wives?

Ravish our daughters? (V.iii.343-365)

~

Here is another chance to compare our adversaries: Richard's speech with its venom and disdain says that the army against them is full of low-lifes. Like Richmond's "if … then" construction, Richard employs phrases of opposites such as his soldiers having both land and beautiful wives while the foe wants to take these away. He sums up his thoughts in the line "If we be conquer'd, let men conquer us," suggesting that the opposing army is not full of men, but "vagabonds," "bastards," and a "milk-sop" or coward, all come over from France to take what belongs to England.

SELECTIONS FROM RICHARD III

COPYWORK 24

SCENE IV. Another part of the field.

Alarum: excursions. Enter NORFOLK and forces fighting; to him CATESBY

CATESBY

Rescue, my Lord of Norfolk, rescue, rescue!

The king enacts more wonders than a man,

Daring an opposite to every danger:

His horse is slain, and all on foot he fights,

Seeking for Richmond in the throat of death.

Rescue, fair lord, or else the day is lost!

Alarums. Enter KING RICHARD III

KING RICHARD III

A horse! a horse! my kingdom for a horse!

CATESBY

Withdraw, my lord; I'll help you to a horse.

KING RICHARD III

Slave, I have set my life upon a cast,

And I will stand the hazard of the die:

I think there be six Richmonds in the field;

Five have I slain to-day instead of him.

A horse! a horse! my kingdom for a horse!

Exeunt (V.iv.1-16)

∾

Scene iii has ended with Richard heading off stage, shouting for St George just as Richmond had been doing (St George is the patron saint of England), and then we have the sudden news that Richard has been unhorsed during battle and is in danger. Catesby offers to help but Richard uses the image of gambling with the idea that he is taking his chances on foot as one would stake a bet on the next roll of a die. He seems to be kind of crazed at this point anyway, probably driven mad by the fact that he has killed a lot of soldiers who disguised themselves as Richmond. One thing I find interesting about this scene with its famous line is that we, the audience, have experienced perhaps a 30-second difference between Richard's heading to battle in the previous scene, and coming onto the stage without his horse in this one, but clearly, this battle has been raging for some time if Richard has been killing so many soldiers in disguise. These are Richard's last words. What follows next is an actual battle or duel between Richard and Richmond where Richard is slain. Since this is the last scene, there isn't a performance issue about having a dead body on stage that can lie there while the final soliloquy is spoken, whereupon finishing, the actor can jump up and take his bow.

SELECTIONS FROM RICHARD III

COPYWORK 25

RICHMOND

Inter their bodies as becomes their births:

Proclaim a pardon to the soldiers fled

That in submission will return to us:

And then, as we have ta'en the sacrament,

We will unite the white rose and the red:

Smile heaven upon this fair conjunction,

That long have frown'd upon their enmity!

What traitor hears me, and says not amen?

England hath long been mad, and scarr'd herself;

The brother blindly shed the brother's blood,

The father rashly slaughter'd his own son,

The son, compell'd, been butcher to the sire:

All this divided York and Lancaster,

Divided in their dire division,

O, now, let Richmond and Elizabeth,

The true succeeders of each royal house,

By God's fair ordinance conjoin together!

And let their heirs, God, if thy will be so.

Enrich the time to come with smooth-faced peace,

With smiling plenty and fair prosperous days!

Abate the edge of traitors, gracious Lord,

That would reduce these bloody days again,

And make poor England weep in streams of blood!

Let them not live to taste this land's increase

That would with treason wound this fair land's peace!

Now civil wounds are stopp'd, peace lives again:

That she may long live here, God say amen!

Exeunt (V.iv.33-58)

∾

The final speech is about reconciliation and closure: those who have been slain, Richmond says, are to be buried, and those who abandoned Richard in battle are to be pardoned. More importantly, the wars of the roses are now finished and Richmond will unite the white and red roses through marrying Elizabeth of the House of York. His claim that they are both the "true succeeders" of their families is stretching the truth (Richmond's claim was shaky at best), but to bid God's blessing on the "fair" and "prosperous days" of their heirs is to invoke Shakespeare's queen, Elizabeth I, whose grandparents these were. To "abate the edge of traitors" is to foil any designs of enemies that may have ideas to rebel, meaning both those in the days following Richmond's victory as well as those perhaps embroiled in conspiracy in the days of Elizabeth's reign. Though she had been on the throne since 1558 and seen off supporters of her sister Mary and those of her cousin, Mary Queen of Scots, she was an aging monarch without heirs, so rebellion was an ever-present threat.

Two final things to say about this last speech: tragedies often end with a lot of deaths and the main character being vanquished, but a line gets drawn under all this trouble with a speech that points toward a return to order. This is what Richmond is doing here. In this particular speech, I like that it ends with the personification of peace and Richmond's saying, "that she may long live here" now that the civil war has been ended. Now go look at line 9 from our first copy-work selection from this play: do you see how Richard personifies war? You may remember he was saying that the battle-time had finished and it was now time for soldiers to woo, though he wasn't good-looking enough to do this. He vows to wage his own private war, but by the end, Richmond's female peace has conquered Richard's male war. Peace is often represented as female, but made even more poignant by having a queen on the throne - Elizabeth was also the peace that, her subjects would hope, would "long live here".

RICHARD III: THE PRODUCTIONS

I have only seen one production of this play, and it was a doozey! Directed by Val May in 1995, it was performed outdoors in the ruins of Ludlow Castle in Shropshire, England, as part of the annual Ludlow Arts Festival (sadly, this festival was axed after 2014).

Two things stood out for me that have made this one of my favourite Shakespeare productions of all time.

First, Ludlow was the actual place of residence for the young princes, Edward and Richard, Edward IV's sons. There is a line in the play where one of the courtiers, Buckingham, says:

Forthwith from Ludlow the young prince be fetch'd

Hither to London, to be crown'd our king.

And here we were, sitting in chairs with those very ruins towering around us ... the place where those young princes had lived, and from where they were taken to their eventual demise.

That sent shivers up our spines.

Also making use of the surroundings to good effect was the scene toward the end where Richard is visited by all the ghosts of people he had killed. It was staged by having the actors stand on the upmost battlements of the castle. This was three storeys above us, with spotlights at their feet to uplight their towering, ghostly, and eerie figures. It was very effective.

Royalty free image from Pixabay

RICHARD III: THE FILMS

I have seen two films of Richard III, and the best is the 1995 version directed by Richard Loncraine and starring Ian McKellen in the title role.

The film is rated "R" (or its equivalent in the UK, a 15), but there is really only one objectionable scene as far as I can tell. As Richard is systematically removing his enemies, he sets his sights on the family of Edward's queen, Elizabeth Woodville. He sees them as upstarts and meddlers, but worse, Elizabeth's brother Anthony, known as Earl Rivers, is the mentor of Edward's young son Edward, and a vehement opponent to Richard's Protectorate during the prince's minority.

Obviously, Richard can't have any obstacles in his way, so he has Earl Rivers murdered.

In the film, this is done by having a woman seduce him in a bedroom, and an assassin skewering him through the mattress.

It isn't bloody or gruesome, but there is strong intimations of a sexual encounter just before his death, and to top it all off, Earl Rivers is played by Robert Downey, Jr.

Tres disastre!!!!

That said, it's an excellent period piece with overtones of 1930s fascism, the Woodvilles portrayed as American, and McKellen the quintessential Machiavellian character of charm and deceit, using one and then the other depending on his purposes for that moment.

~

The second film of Richard III is the made-for-tv adaptation by the BBC in the Hollow Crown: Wars of the Roses series (Cycle 2 from 2016). Richard is played by Benedict Cumberbatch throughout the trilogy, starting as a young, misshapen man in Henry VI Part 1, and becoming more vile and evil as the series progresses.

However, as much as I love Cumberbatch, I do not recommend this second series (the first series or "Cycle 1" from 2012 that portrays Richard II to Henry V is superb). It is very violent and graphic with beheadings and sexual encounters that my teen son found so disturbing that he left the room.

We were very shocked at the Cycle 2 production after enjoying Cycle 1 so much.

AFTERWORD

I hope you have learned a lot from this little taste of Shakespeare. I think the best way to experience him is to read as many of his plays as one can, see as many productions as one can, and spend some time in deliberate copywork as modeled in this book, mainly for the purpose of highlighting the echoes, repetitions, and connections between texts. These add both to the enjoyment and the mastery of understanding his works.

It is my intention to continue breaking down Shakespeare's plays for purposes of copywork, understanding, and connection, but for now, I have begun with a comedy and a history-cum-tragedy. I doubt they will be enough.

"'Tis true," Othello says, "there's magic in the web of it." He speaks of an enchanted cloak, but I speak of the way that Shakespeare weaves his words.

Magic.

Printed in Poland
by Amazon Fulfillment
Poland Sp. z o.o., Wrocław